Astronauts in Space

LEVEL 6

Written by: Caroline Laidlaw
Series Editor: Melanie Williams

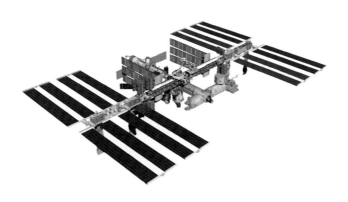

Pearson Education Limited
Edinburgh Gate, Harlow,
Essex CM20 2JE, England
and Associated Companies throughout the world.

ISBN: 978-1-4082-8847-4

This edition first published by Pearson Education Ltd 2014
7 9 10 8
Text copyright © Pearson Education Ltd 2014

The moral rights of the author have been asserted
in accordance with the Copyright Designs and Patents Act 1988

Set in 15/19pt OT Fiendstar
Printed in Slovakia by Neografia

Acknowledgements

The publisher would like to thank the following for their kind permission to reproduce their photographs:
(Key: b-bottom; c-centre; l-left; r-right; t-top)

Alamy Images: Christopher Stewart 4b, NASA Archive 17t; **Corbis:** 27, NASA / Reuters 28, NASA / Roger Ressmeyer 29br; **Fotolia.com:** Zhanna Ocheret 5; **IBMP:** SSC RF IBMP RAS 35tl, 35bl; **NASA:** 3cl, 3cr, 3bl, 6, 11, 12, 13, 14, 16, 17b, 18t, 19br, 20b, 21t, 21b, 22t, 22b, 24t, 25, 26l, 30b, 31tr, 31c, 32, 33t, 33b, 34b, MIT Professor Dava Newman: Inventor, Science Engineering; Guillermo Trotti, A.I.A., Trotti and Associates, Inc. (Cambridge, MA): Design; Dainese (Vincenca, Italy): Fabrication; Douglas Sonders: Photography 18br; **PhotoDisc:** StockTrek 19bl, 34tr; **Science Photo Library Ltd:** European Space Agency 35cr, NASA 15, 20tr, 29c, 30t, RIA Novosti 19t; **Shutterstock. com:** Unique Light 4 (background); **TopFoto:** 1999 TophamPicturepoint 23, AP 7, Fine Art Images / Heritage-Images 9t, RIA Novosti 8tr, 8b, 9b, The Granger Collection 3br, 10
Cover images: *Front:* **NASA**; *Back:* **NASA**

All other images © Pearson Education

Every effort has been made to trace the copyright holders and we apologise in advance
for any unintentional omissions. We would be pleased to insert the appropriate
acknowledgement in any subsequent edition of this publication.

Illustrations: Janos Jantner

Published by Pearson Education Ltd

For a complete list of the titles available in the Pearson English Kids Readers series, please go to
www.pearsonenglishkidsreaders.com. Alternatively, write to your local Pearson Education office or to
Pearson English Readers Marketing Department, Pearson Education, Edinburgh Gate, Harlow, Essex CM202JE, England.

Contents

Looking at the Night Sky

Since the earliest times, people have looked up at the stars, the moon and the planets. In those days, people lived outside most of the time. Because there were no towns or cities, there were no lights at night. The sky looked darker then.

telescope

Today people use telescopes to look at the sky. Thousands of years ago they could only use their eyes. Perhaps they dreamed of leaving Earth and exploring the universe.

Do modern humans see the same night sky which early people saw? Yes, but there are also new things to see. Low-flying planes have bright lights, and people often see orbiting satellites which look like moving stars. A person from the past might say, 'How amazing! What are those lights? Did they come from another planet?'

Modern people do not have impossible dreams about going into space because today space exploration is really happening. People can train to become astronauts and work on a space station which orbits the Earth. They could also join a future mission to the moon or to Mars.

The moon looks bigger and brighter through a telescope.

The First Astronauts

When did humans first go into space? The story began not so very long ago, but the first astronauts were not people, they were animals.

Scientists wanted to make space exploration as safe as possible for humans. So they decided to experiment with animals and test them in unmanned spaceflights. Insects, mice, frogs, dogs and monkeys were some of the animals which first went into space. Many died. We should remember these animals and thank them. They helped to make space exploration safer for humans.

Albert II was the first monkey to go into space, in 1949. He died after his spacecraft landed.

A rocket takes Albert II into space.

Luckily it was different for Ham the Chimp. His story ended happily when he returned to Earth in very good health.

Scientists wanted to know the answer to an important question: could Ham do the same things in spaceflight which he could do on Earth? The answer came in 1961 when Ham went on the Mercury-Redstone 2 mission. Yes, he did everything well and lived for another 16 years.

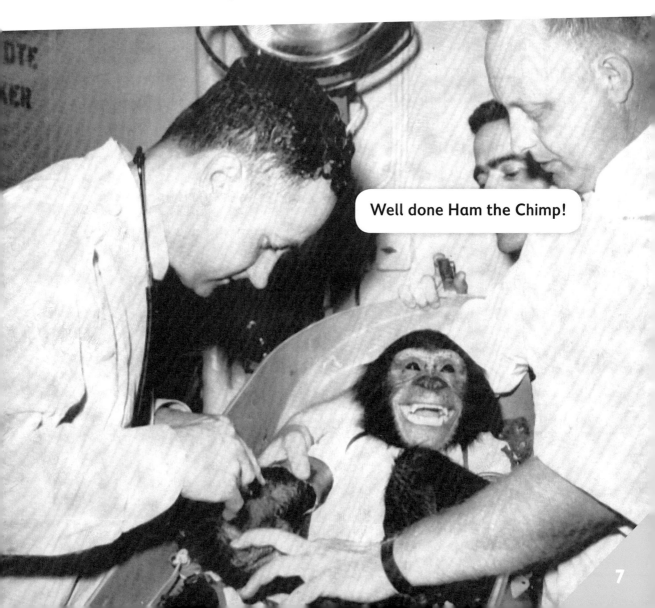

Well done Ham the Chimp!

Sputnik

In 1957, the Soviet Union surprised the whole world when it launched Sputnik 1 into orbit around the Earth. It was the world's first satellite. A month later the Soviet Union launched its second satellite, Sputnik 2. It was a metal ball which weighed 113 kilograms, and it carried a dog.

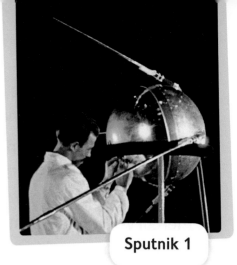

Sputnik 1

The name of this small astronaut was Laika and she had a strange life. Her first home was on the streets of Moscow where she belonged to no-one. Her second home was with scientists who trained her for the Sputnik 2 mission. The saddest part of the story happened after the launch – Laika only lived a few hours.

Laika

The space race

Laika's flight was the beginning of a race between the USA and the Soviet Union. Both countries wanted to be the first to send a man into space.

In 1961 the Soviets won this race when Yuri Gagarin became the first man in space. His spacecraft, Vostok 1, completed one Earth orbit.

Yuri Gagarin

Valentina Tereshkova

Two years later, in 1963, Valentina Tereshkova from the Soviet Union became the first woman in space. Her flight took nearly 80 hours and she flew 48 times around the Earth.

Apollo 11

On 16 July 1969, the eyes of the world were watching the USA when a Saturn 5 rocket launched the Command Module (Columbia) and the Lunar Module (Eagle) into space. Inside Columbia, there were three astronauts, Commander Michael Collins, Neil Armstrong and Buzz Aldrin. Three and a half days later, Neil Armstrong became the first man to walk on the moon.

Apollo 11 launch

Armstrong and Aldrin were on the moon for 21 hours, but they spent only two and a half hours exploring the moon's surface. Here they found rocks and moon dust to take back to Earth for scientific experiments.

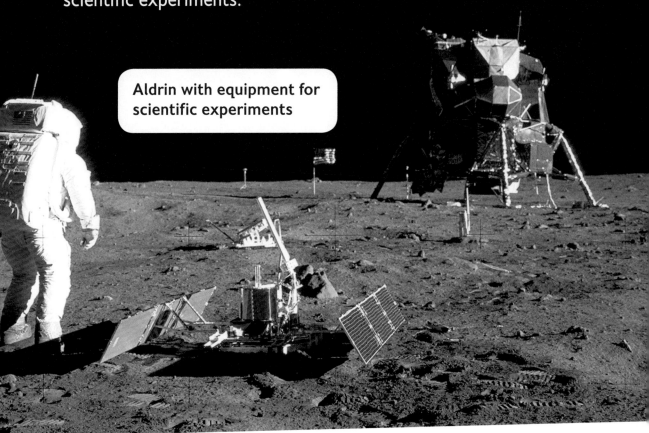

Aldrin with equipment for scientific experiments

When Armstrong and Aldrin were busy on the moon, Commander Collins was orbiting in Columbia. He was waiting for the other two astronauts to finish their work. When Armstrong and Aldrin were ready, they launched themselves off the moon in Eagle, then docked with Columbia. After that, the three astronauts returned to Earth, but they left Eagle behind. Two years later it fell from orbit onto the moon.

Earth looks very small from the surface of the moon.

Getting around on the moon

After Apollo 11, five more missions took men to the moon. On the first three missions, the astronauts moved around on foot. It was a slow way to travel because walking in spacesuits is not easy. Thick dust and rocks cover the surface. The astronauts explored only a few hundred metres around their spacecraft.

In July 1971, two years after the first moon landing, Apollo 15 took a vehicle to the moon. It was called the Lunar Rover – a kind of open car which made life easier for astronauts to get around. They could explore much more of the moon's surface in the Lunar Rover. It carried scientific equipment and had a camera at the front. Lunar Rovers also went to the moon on the Apollo 16 and 17 missions.

In December 1972, Apollo 17 astronauts, Ronald Evans and Harrison Schmitt, were the last men on the moon. They drove 30.5 kilometres and spent 75 hours there. They took 110 kilograms of rocks and dust back to Earth.

Exploring the moon's surface on Lunar Rover

Future space exploration

American engineers are developing a Space Exploration Vehicle (SEV). If there is a return mission to the moon, astronauts will be able to live and work inside the vehicle. They will wear their Earth clothes inside, but outside they will have to wear spacesuits. The first Lunar Rover was really just an open car. The SEV will be closed and will look different.

The USA and China might send astronauts to the moon sometime in the future. Their astronauts will probably explore hundreds of kilometres of the moon's surface.

Staying Alive in Space

Humans have lived on Earth for many thousands of years. We breathe its air, drink its water and we eat the food which grows here. In space, there is no air, no water and no food. If astronauts do not take supplies of these important things on space flights, they will die.

The environment inside a modern spacecraft has everything which a person needs to stay alive. But it is not exactly the same as it is on Earth because inside an orbiting spacecraft everything floats.

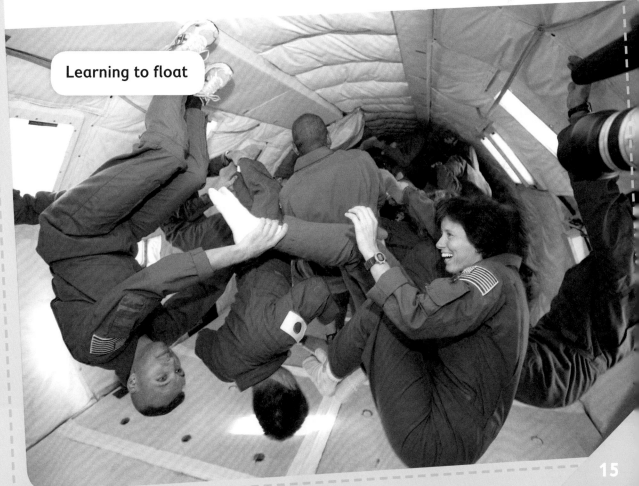

Learning to float

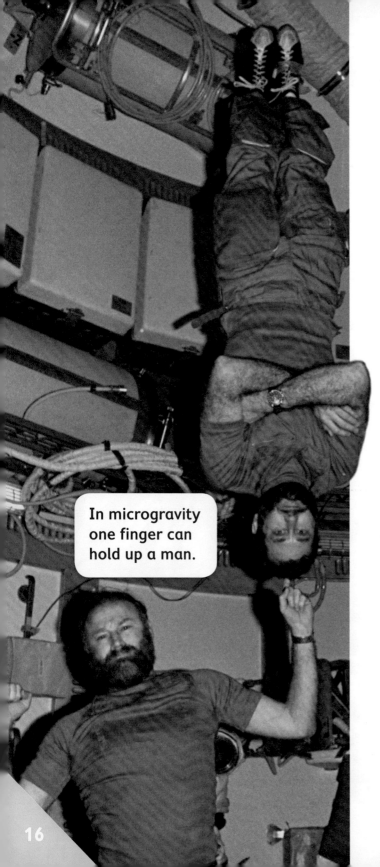

In microgravity one finger can hold up a man.

Why don't people and things float on Earth? It is because the Earth's gravity holds us to the ground. Gravity is a force which keeps the moon in orbit around the Earth and the planets in orbit around the sun.

Gravity also pulls an orbiting spacecraft towards the Earth. In fact, the spacecraft is in free-fall, but its speed keeps it in orbit. The spacecraft and everything and everyone inside are falling at the same speed. Free-falling produces a microgravity environment in which everything floats and seems to be weightless.

Spacesuits

An astronaut outside a spacecraft must wear a spacesuit to stay alive. The space environment can be too hot or too cold, but the spacesuit keeps the body at the right temperature. It carries air for the astronauts to breathe and water for them to drink during an Extravehicular Activity (EVA), which is the name for a spacewalk or moonwalk.

Sound does not travel in space, so astronauts use equipment inside their spacesuits to communicate with each other.

spacesuit

Aldrin's spacesuit was slow to put on and difficult to wear.

Modern spacesuits, or Extravehicular Mobility Units (EMUs), are much easier to wear.

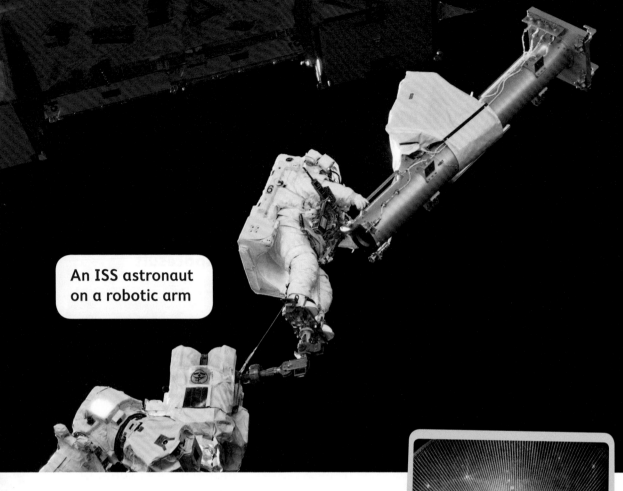

An ISS astronaut on a robotic arm

Astronauts use tethers on EMUs to attach themselves to space stations. If a tether breaks and an astronaut floats away, he or she can use the EMU's life jacket to fly back to the station. Sometimes, when astronauts work outside, they stand on a robotic arm.

What will spacesuits of the future look like? Professor Dava Newman is leading research on the BioSuit which is light and easy to move in. Maybe one day astronauts will wear BioSuits on Mars.

Dava Newman wears the BioSuit.

The First Space Stations

Salyut 1

In 1971 the Soviet Union launched Salyut 1. It was the world's first orbiting space station. Later, three astronauts went in a Soyuz spacecraft to join Salyut 1 for 24 days.

Soyuz

Salyut

The Soyuz spacecraft docks with Salyut 1.

Skylab

America's first space station went into orbit in 1973. On this mission, three astronauts did different kinds of scientific experiments and studied the Earth below. They also did tests on human health in space.

Skylab above the Earth

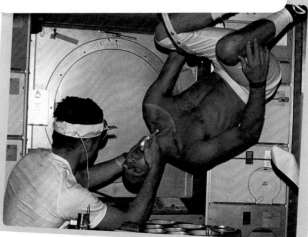

The astronaut does not need a chair for a tooth examination in Skylab.

Mir

The Soviet Union launched Mir in 1986, and it stayed in orbit for 15 years. During that time, Mir grew bigger and bigger. Why did that happen? Scientists wanted to build a home where astronauts could live, and a science laboratory where they could work. Bit by bit they sent new modules to fit onto Mir.

Mir was the first space station in which Soviet and American astronauts lived and worked together. The American Space Shuttle took astronauts to Mir, and carried supplies.

Mir orbits the Earth.

Space Shuttle Atlantis docks with Mir for the first time in 1995.

The Space Shuttle Programme

NASA's Space Shuttle was a kind of space lorry which could go into space and come back again. Before the Space Shuttle programme, a spacecraft could do only one mission, but Shuttles could go and come back many times.

A Space Shuttle launch

A lorry carries things from one place to another. The Shuttle was exactly that, but it carried things into space. It carried new satellites to put into orbit, and equipment for repairing old satellites.

NASA had five Space Shuttles – Columbia, Challenger, Discovery, Atlantis and Endeavour.

A Space Shuttle landing

In 1990, Space Shuttle Discovery put the Hubble space telescope into orbit 569 kilometres above the Earth. The telescope was the size of a city bus. Not long afterwards, NASA ground control discovered a problem. Hubble was not working. It was sending pictures back to Earth which were not clear. So in 1993 Shuttle Endeavour took astronauts to repair the telescope in space. First they caught it and attached it to the Shuttle. Then the repair work could begin. A robotic arm helped with this job which took five days to complete.

The Hubble space telescope

After the repair, Hubble started taking beautifully clear pictures of the universe.

A Hubble photo of a galaxy where stars are born.

Between the first launch on 12 April, 1981 and the last landing back on Earth on 21 July, 2011, Space Shuttles flew 135 missions. During these missions, Shuttle astronauts and space scientists did 75 experiments in Shuttle Spacelabs. They also repaired satellites and helped to build the International Space Station.

Most of NASA's missions have gone well, but space exploration is dangerous. The astronauts on Space Shuttle Challenger died in a terrible accident after its launch on 28 January, 1986.

The International Space Station (ISS)

High above the Earth a group of people live and work in an orbiting laboratory. Their home travels at 32,410 kilometres an hour, at a height of about 400 kilometres. It completes 15 orbits every day.

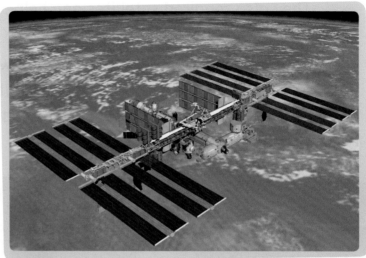

The ISS is a little bigger than a football field.

Astronauts first began building the International Space Station in 1998 when Russia launched the first module. Thirteen years later, after many Space Shuttle missions, astronauts finished building the ISS. It is now big enough for seven people to work, play, exercise and sleep in. They usually spend six months on the space station.

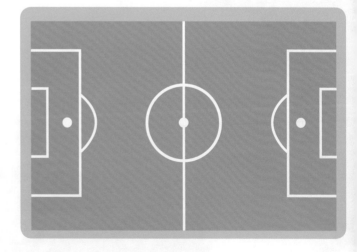

At first, robotic arms did much of the building. Now they do repairs and move astronauts around safely during spacewalks. Robotic arms also lift and move supplies when they arrive from Earth.

Fifteen countries send equipment, astronauts and scientists to work on the ISS. They do important research to develop new medicines. They find out how plants grow in space, and they do other work which can help our planet and its people.

Robotic arms on the ISS

When astronauts first arrive at the ISS, life feels strange. In this email an astronaut describes her life.

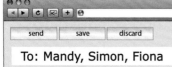

send   save   discard

To: Mandy, Simon, Fiona

From: Betty

Subject: News from space

Hello everyone!

I arrived a few days ago and I've been very busy. I'm fine and I'm enjoying life up here. Being in a microgravity environment is very strange, but it's a lot of fun. I'll try to explain.

The first thing to remember is that things don't fall if you drop them. Just now I dropped my pencil so I looked for it near my feet. It wasn't there because it was floating right next to me! Astronauts often play floating games just for fun!

If you're thinking that I only play up here, you're wrong! My experiment with salad plants in microgravity is going well. I spend hours on computers too! Sometimes I look at the view of Earth below. Then I can't stop looking – it's just so beautiful from here. Yesterday I saw North Africa and the Spanish coast. Somewhere down there is the Spanish village where we went last year. Amazing! I'll write again soon.

Betty

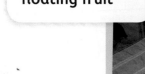

Astronauts with floating fruit

The Spanish and North African coasts from space

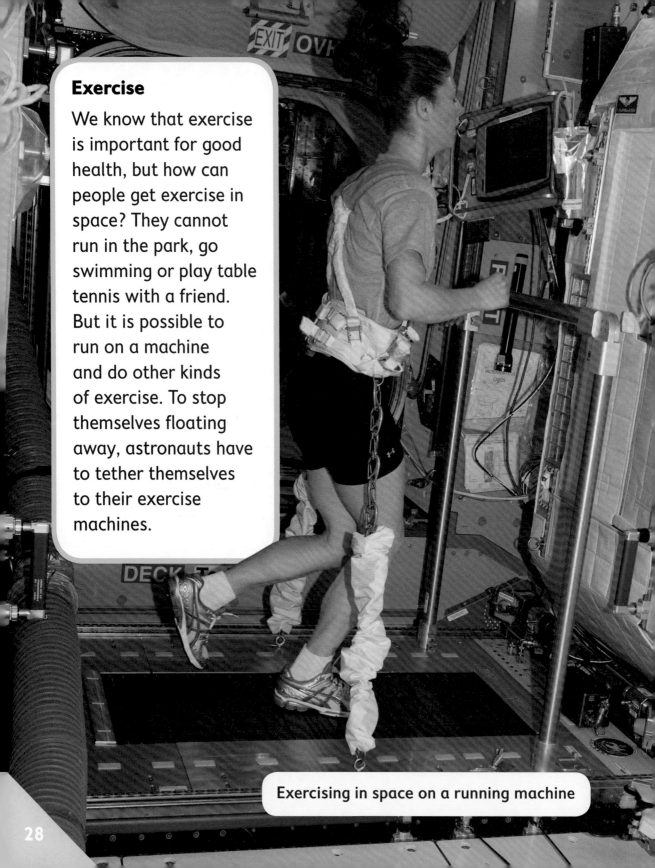

Exercise

We know that exercise is important for good health, but how can people get exercise in space? They cannot run in the park, go swimming or play table tennis with a friend. But it is possible to run on a machine and do other kinds of exercise. To stop themselves floating away, astronauts have to tether themselves to their exercise machines.

Exercising in space on a running machine

Sleeping

When astronauts are living on a space station, they have to forget about Earth nights and days. They are in a satellite which flies around the Earth once every 90 minutes. This means that the sun rises 15 times in 24 hours. Imagine if you had to go to bed 15 times a day!

Astronauts usually sleep in bags.

Astronauts follow Earth times for day and night, so they cover their eyes and get into sleeping bags when they are tired. They must remember to attach their sleeping bags to a hard surface or they will wake up somewhere else!

Not all astronauts sleep in bags. In space there is no 'up' or 'down' so you can sleep on your head if you want.

Food

There are hundreds of different kinds of bags on the space station – big ones for sleeping in, and small ones for keeping food in. Food in bags usually needs warm water to prepare it for eating.

Space food in plastic bags

Meals were not very good in the early days of space exploration, but now they are much better. On the ISS astronauts can choose to eat food from many different countries.

Some astronauts prefer eating their food out of plastic bags. Others like to hold it in their hands. Tortillas are much more popular than bread which breaks easily, floats away and gets lost in equipment.

tortilla

Staying clean

Astronauts use a kind of soap which does not need water to wash off. They must not let any of the soap float away, so they use towels to dry themselves quickly.

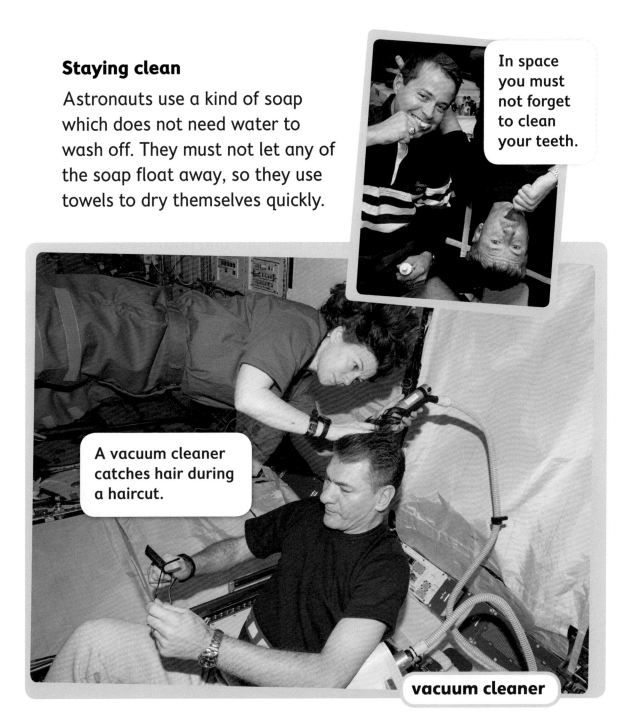

In space you must not forget to clean your teeth.

A vacuum cleaner catches hair during a haircut.

vacuum cleaner

A vacuum cleaner keeps dust out of equipment. It is also very useful for catching things which float and are difficult to reach.

Training to be an Astronaut

It takes many years of study and hard work even before you start astronaut training. First you must study a science subject or medicine. If you want to be a spaceflight engineer you must also learn to be a pilot.

It helps if you speak English and Russian because many countries work together on space missions and both these languages are useful.

Training in a deep pool

You must also be able to work well in a team, or alone when it is necessary. You must also be able to act quickly if anything goes wrong.

At last, after all this preparation, you are ready to start

training. In Europe future astronauts can train at the European Astronaut Centre (EAC) in Germany. You can also train in Russia, Canada, America and Japan.

Space training centres teach future astronauts about many different kinds of missions. Students can practise being

weightless in deep pools of water with spacecraft modules. Pools cannot give students a real microgravity environment, but they can prepare students for living and working in microgravity.

The Future of Space Travel

Mission to Mars

Space scientists have sent men and vehicles to the moon and unmanned spacecraft into deep space. They have put a space laboratory in orbit around the Earth.

Now scientists are preparing to send astronauts to our nearest planet, Mars. They have already landed Curiosity Rover, which is an unmanned exploration vehicle. Before astronauts can land on Mars, there is an important question to answer.

Mars

Curiosity Rover

A space garden

Will astronauts' minds and bodies stay healthy on a lonely journey which takes 18 months? The Mars-500 Project tried to answer this question.

Scientists put a group of six men in a spacecraft on the ground in Russia for a 520-day 'flight' to Mars and back. During this time, the scientists did not see their families or anyone else for 18 months. They tried not to worry, but to keep busy. There was plenty to do. They grew plants, did tests on themselves, and played music and computer games in their free time.

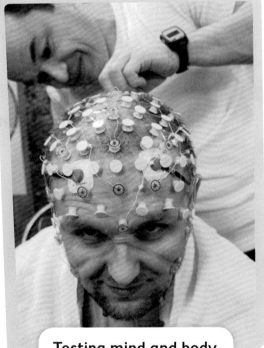

Testing mind and body

At the end of the 'journey' to Mars and back again, engineer Romain Charles said that he travelled millions of kilometres without moving a single centimetre!

Holidays in space

A possible business plan for the future is to put a hotel in orbit around the Earth. Perhaps there will be visits to the moon from the hotel. Or people may prefer to stay on the hotel to watch the Earth below and to play games in microgravity. The hotel will have comfortable rooms, but no showers, and food will be the kind which astronauts eat on the ISS. Space tourists will have to be healthy, and they will have to train for a few months before going into space. They will also have to be rich.

An idea for an orbiting space hotel

An idea for a future space station

Future space stations

Two hundred years ago, many Europeans went to live on the other side of the world. Their journey took many weeks. They felt that they were in another world, and communication by letter was very slow. In the future, people might go even further and live on space stations.

Travelling is much faster now and communication happens in real time. Would you like to live on a space station? Or would you prefer to live on Earth, but work in space?

Glossary

dock (v) page 11 — to join with another vehicle in space

equipment (n) page 11 — the thing or things which you need to do a job

experiment (n and v) page 6 — testing an idea to find out about something

float (v) page 15 — to move around freely in the air

galaxy (n) page 22 — a very big group of stars

gravity (n) page 16 — a force which makes bodies fall to the ground or which pulls things together

laboratory (n) page 20 — a place where scientists do experiments

launch (n and v) page 8 — to send something on its way at the beginning of a journey

microgravity (adj and n) page 16 — free-fall produces a microgravity environment in which people and things seem to be weightless, and they float

mission (n) page 5 — an important job for a person or group of people

module (n) page 10 — one part of a spacecraft

orbit (n and v) page 5 — the path which a moon, planet or spacecraft follows when it travels around another body in space

research (n) page 18 — studying facts to find answers to questions which people ask

spacecraft (n) page 6 — a vehicle which travels in space

universe (n) page 4 — the Earth, the Solar System, the galaxies and everything in space

unmanned (spaceflight or spacecraft) (adj) page 6 — without a person or people inside

vehicle (n) page 13 — a machine which moves people and things from one place to another

Activity page ❶

Before You Read

You can use a dictionary to do these activities.

1 **What is this book about? Look at the cover.**
Answer *Yes*, *No* or *Maybe*.

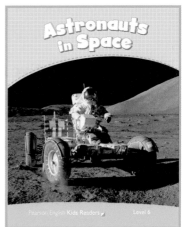

  a Actors and films about life on
     other planets.
  b People who live and work in airports.
  c People who live and work in space.
  d Museums about space.
  e Information about space exploration.

2 **Look at these pages and answer the questions.**

  a Page 11 – Is the astronaut wearing clothes or a spacesuit?
     Is he standing next to equipment or furniture?
  b Page 15 – Are these people walking or floating? Are they
     weightless or heavy?
  c Page 20 – Are these vehicles or buildings? Are they spacecraft
     or boats?

Activity page 2

After You Read

1 Choose adjectives which best describe astronauts.

> healthy   strong   stupid   intelligent
> brave   funny   careful   scared

2 Choose adjectives which best describe astronauts' work.

> boring   lonely   strange   difficult
> interesting   dangerous   easy   frightening

3 Match the two halves of the sentences.

1 The Hubble	**a** is a vehicle on Mars.
2 Yuri Gagarin	**b** was the first man to walk on the moon.
3 The ISS	**c** is a kind of spacesuit.
4 Neil Armstrong	**d** was the first man to orbit the Earth.
5 Curiosity Rover	**e** is a space telescope.
6 An EMU	**f** is an orbiting laboratory.

4 Imagine you are an astronaut. You are visiting the ISS for 24 hours. Write a short letter to your family or friends.

Is life the same as it is on Earth?

What can you see through the windows?

What do you like doing, or not like doing?